52 Sundays

ISBN-13: 978-1-7333008-0-3
ISBN-10: 1-7333008-0-5

Dear Reader,

What you are about to read is a collection of poetry I wrote during the first year of my beloved grandmothers cancer diagnosis. This has been both a tragic and trying time for my family. At the time I am writing this…God willing, my grandmother is still alive. I hope this book makes her proud. If you have ever sat beside someone you love suffering with cancer then you are well aware that unfortunately, you prematurely go through the 7 stages of grief before your loved one has even passed, in preparation for the worst. I wrote this book to express what I was feeling and the plethora of undesirable thoughts that flooded my mind. Thank you for reading and a big thank you to my incredible family.

I wrote this for you. For me. For us.
You are my sunshine…

Shock
and
Denial

Melanie Ann Vangas

I saw her bones beneath her bata.
There was a rattle in her cough.
When the bones
and rattle
        lingered for months
I knew it was time.
But she h a t e d the doctor.
Maybe because she knew
that he would know
something we hadn't (yet).

- Symptoms.

"They found a mass on my adrenal gland".
I ran to my room.
Hung up the phone.
Nearly lost my life.
Thinking of a day without you seemed…
unreasonable,
unacceptable,
impossible.
I spread the news and easily discredited
everybody else's pain
because they didn't love you like I did.
They weren't your soulmates.
I was
you
reincarnated
while you were still here.

 - I don't know what I'll do if she has cancer // I can't lose
her.

I'm afraid to miss something
I so desperately want to say.

\-   Urgency and forgetfulness.

I have this fear that once I'm done
spilling my pain to paper
the story will be over.

This story cannot be over.

-   Superstition.

Melanie Ann Vangas

You were admitted.
We had been there a few days.
Us and your best friend.
Us and your soulmate.

You see, we haven't spent much time together…
but as I'm older and can witness you two in dialogue,
in sync,
in life and love,
I grow to love her nearly as much as I love you;
I'm thankful for that.

Because the night she prayed
above your bed
I had no shame in
pouring
bursting
releasing
as she held my shoulder
and wiped my cheeks.
Everything felt like it was going to be okay.
Glory be to God.
-   J&T, A&B.

52 Sundays

When I first found out
I couldn't decide if
I wanted to pour my heart out
or if I wanted to be
your knight in shining armor.

A heavy weight to carry,
deciding whether to be
your saving grace
or a burden.

- Can I cry or should I just wipe your tears?

Something about this nightmare
tells me that it's happening to prove to me that God is real.
Something about this nightmare
seems temporary.

It's not stupidity, it's not being naive.
I am not hopeful.
Something is whispering to my bones
that you are going to be okay.
You will overcome this.
Remission and all.
Something is telling me
to listen for your heartbeat…
as it is nowhere near over.

- You must live on for the both of us.

The four of us were in one room.
Quaint and private, for a treatment cubicle.
I hadn't been to one of your treatments
in over half of a year.
Things were going so well
and you had your hunny by your side.

If I could describe to you what it felt like to be swallowed
by misery and eternity all at once.

I probably wouldn't dare.
"I wanted to make you better but treatment doesn't seem
to be working.
I'm sorry."

- Another mindless, senseless, emotionless, insensitive,
  uneducated Oncologist.

Melanie Ann Vangas

I booked a trip to Arizona.
I feel filthy and pained
because it's the one place
we wanted to travel to together.
Just to make matters more crucial,
it's booked it for October.
Your birth month.
Part of me is at peace because
I hope that you can make it.
Morbid, sad me is at peace because
I know that you will make it, regardless.

- Ashes, ashes. We all fall down..

Blurry.
Drowning.

Tears were swallowing your eyeballs.

I watched you shake with fear.
Breathing
        quickly
                now.
I have no idea what it's like
to feel the grim reaper
breathe
down
your
neck.

It is not fair that you must face death.

Maybe I'm naive.
But Death will not win.

I am here.

-   You do not have to be afraid.

Melanie Ann Vangas

We all dream of you often.
Who you were before, that is.
Partially in preparation,
partially in denial.
I cling on to the tone of your voice,
your posture,
your habits,
the way you walk,
put rollers in your hair,
laugh,
etc.

-   Reminiscent.

An earthquake hit
and destroyed our village.

Devastation
engulfed
the ground beneath us.

It was then that we learned,
that all
   we have
      is each other.

All
we
need.

– Fuck Cancer.

At first we trusted his experience and expertise.
However, there was something unsettling
about listening to a man
who would blatantly encourage the end of life
quicker than usual.
It seemed he was bitter,
as his own mother did not win her battle.

You would encourage patients to fight.
But Doctors don't believe in miracles.
They believe in science.

Something was unsettling about
him so easily asking you to your face
what you wanted.
It seemed distasteful.

It hurt when he took your
"I don't want to be in any pain"
as a goodbye.

I died a little inside hearing my grandfather,
our own patriarch,
ask us to leave the room
and violently,
passively
close the door.
A pastor knocked
and he rejected his presence.

A spirit was broken that day

But I am glad to say
that in the end,
It was not my bloodline.

Prick.

- Dr. K

We were reassured it could very well
just be a cyst.

We have to get a second opinion.

We *have to* get a second opinion.

- They must have gotten it wrong.

I was convinced

that you would make up

the less than 10%

that survived.

- You're going to beat this.

Just a little

    while

        longer.

I need her

    just a little

        while

            longer.

-   What I whisper. 24/7.

Pain
and
Guilt

Don't you worry…
I'll still be sure to wave from inside of the car
bring my pointer finger to my eye

"I"

close my fingers together and form the curve of
a heart against my chest

"love"

point his way

"you"

and honk twice
everytime I pull out of the driveway.

- Traditions.

I'm wasting time mourning the loss of you
when it has not happened yet.
Preparing myself
with wound kits
for the pain I know will kill me.
Mourning,
grieving,
the loss
of you,
the death of you.

- Why am I so pessimistic?

Melanie Ann Vangas

Stern and influential…
your voice sounded
just like old times
as we sat on the couch
and watched our "trash TV".

Momentarily, I forgot
that we were living in this nightmare.

Then in an unfamiliar tone of voice,
you said, supple and child-like,
that there was a case against you.
That you had raped someone and they were after you.

//

You asked if your tattoos were removable
and when I asked which tattoos you had on your
bare and dainty body
you replied "the tear drops down my eyes".

I have never been slapped so violently.
- Ripping normality from my gut // Brain Lesions

I fear
yet, am comforted by
our connection.

Telepathically,
physically,
spiritually,
eternally…

So I brace myself
for the faint sensation of death,
the moment you take your last breath.
Something tells me
as you go
I will follow.

- Together forever and always.

Melanie Ann Vangas

Today was serene.
I say this because I convinced myself
to enjoy my new patio furniture.

I say this because the quiet wind
blew my hair out of my eyes
after kissing my forehead.
I say this because I grabbed my book
and my wine
and everything felt normal.

There was something about the scent.
The pleasant, green scent
that washed up old memories
of us by the lake, us by the pool, us on the patio.

My evening felt cinematic.
Then came the punch in my gut.
Knocked the wind and tears right out of me.
Reminding me that one day I will,
without choice
have to do these things without you.

- Randomly.

I don't think I could ever thank you
                    enough.

For a lot of things...
But for right now, fighting
              with all of your might
to stay alive for the sake of us
because you know that we need you, desperately.

I can't imagine my body betraying me,
failing on me.
Still you wake up with an inhale and a smile
that
wonderful,
beautiful,
smile...
to stay alive for the sake of us.

- Just incase I haven't said "Thank You".

Melanie Ann Vangas

The weirdest thing is
grieving the loss of someone
who is still here.

- Is this a part of the process?

26

52 Sundays

Every time my phone rings
and I see it comes from your home
or my grandfather
or my aunts

my heart stops beating.

-   Please, not yet.

Melanie Ann Vangas

Leaving her to care for you felt wrong.
She must have figured out her own routine
throughout the week.
I came to see how things were going…
the giant elephant in the room kept me away.

How could I sit and watch someone
who wasn't me
feed you, change you, roll you on your side?

You see, I knew
we were comfortable with one another.
I knew how to gently care for you.
I could talk you through changing the sheets
and remind you that you were safe in my arms when we
turned you.
I could send love through your aura.
I could whisper and you'd feel comfort.

I didn't even want to see
what was happening
     w i t h o u t   m e.

- No one takes care of you like I do.

52 Sundays

I had gone away for a weekend
then I had to resume to normal, societal tasks
like working and working on friendships.
The first night was the toughest.
I could hardly sleep
without knowing you were near.

Upon my return, you hardly acknowledged me.
Were you mad at me for leaving?
For leaving someone else to care for you?
For going about my life
while yours was at a stand still?

- Guilt.

I do not care what riches are waiting for me.

Currency could never compensate

for how poor I will feel

without you.

- You were thinking it, I said it // "Trust fund babies".

52 Sundays

Some days
I am a warrior
and you, my General.
You have fought through trenches
for your scars.
Un defeat-able.

Some days

I sulk.

- It comes and goes in waves.

Melanie Ann Vangas

Admittedly, it has been disheartening...

To watch a man who had his entire life planned
with the woman he loves
fall apart.

It has been painful
to witness him
muster up the courage
to swim out into a lonely
oasis

only to watch him drown

in tears he's choked back

for
quite
some
time
now.

- He is lost without you.

2:37 AM.
It's a Monday.
Not to mention
I have effortlessly downed a bottle of wine.

This is becoming a ritual
since I can't sleep anymore.

My, I know this is what you were afraid of.

- I hope I wake up in time for work this morning.

Melanie Ann Vangas

If I am being honest,

I am scared for you.

Inevitably we are born and we die.
I've never had a seat this close
to this stage at this show that I never want to end
but when it does,
will it hurt?
Will you feel? Pain? Emotions?
Will you cry?
Will you see white?
Does your life really flash ahead of you?
Will the memories comfort you or
will your soul grasp a tight grip
torturously being ripped from them?
Will you remember my name?
Or how much I loved you?
Will you always be right beside me?

- I'd hate to think of us always together in parallel
  universe.

52 Sundays

Writing this has felt like
a sword slicing through my flesh
and abrasively sawing through my bones.
From head to toe.

- It h u r t s .

Melanie Ann Vangas

You were being so strong
and I sat there with a puss of my face.
A gaping hole in my heart,
selfishly.
I wasn't the one who was dying.

It took months for me to be able to look at you
without having panic attacks.
That wasn't fair.
So I'm left with
"Did I make it worse?".
I should have been celebrating life with you
making you laugh,
asking you to tell me stories,
more about yourself.
I should have been your saving grace.
Instead I hid behind four walls
in a dark and gloomy place.
Isolated.

And that wasn't fair.
I wasn't the one who was dying.

-   The nerve of me.

Not even coffee tasted the same when

it wasn't your dainty fingers

and feminine demise

making it.

- Nothing will ever be the same.

Melanie Ann Vangas

My biggest wish is that you can somehow
translate from mind to paper
a manual
a timeline
a plan for my life ahead.
Truly, I have expected this of you all along.
So naturally it's strange for me to think of planning my
own life ahead.
You had all the answers, all the dreams.
I had no idea where I was going.
I trusted you
and your instinct and your opinion.
I valued you
and your wishes and desires for my life.
I had this gut feeling that I would be,
I would be successful in the end
as long as I blindly, passionately followed you.

Now that the blind fold has been ripped off
I'm not sure what steps to take.

- Lost.

This week came with lots of rain.

I had tons of time to create.

Poetry,

videos,

depression.

- I wonder if we will make magic this week? June 2019.

I never knew

if it was proper etiquette

to cry in-front of

a cancer patient.

- Choking on my tears.

I am hurt.
I am angry.

at you.

Because of all of the lessons…
    of all of the things you taught me

you forgot to teach me

how
to
live
without
you.

- Survival and existence.

I wanted to ask you so many things.
I wanted to know it all.

Like your favorite color
your first time riding a bike
how your very first interview went
your drunken high school stories
how you picked your jewelry out
made decisions on your investments
your choice in interior design
where you saw my future headed
your deepest desires
what you felt like you missed out on in life during
your 67 years here
what hurt the most
who your childhood enemies were
more about my family
why you loved cardinals
how you worked through your biggest fight
with my grandfather
what you thought my future girlfriend would embody

which wedding dress looked the best
what qualities you value about a person
your favorite foods
your favorite recipe
your favorite place

But I didn't want to ask those things.
It felt like once I knew it all,
there would be no more secrets left to tell.
Signifying your time to go.

I was
so
scared
of losing you
I kept the questions to myself.

- I didn't want you to feel like you were dying.

I spent most of that summer

in wine and in booze

because it healed my wounds quicker

than gauze

and God.

- The second summer.

Dominican Republic.
We've been there a thousand times together.
I always admired the way the language
rolled right off your tongue.
We spent our days chasing
Parisian beach wraps
larimar jewelry
mantequilla de maní.

This really is catastrophic.

- What I'd do for one more vacation with you.

I'm sorry

for all of the phone calls that went unanswered
for all of the holidays I've missed
for going more than a month without seeing you
for making you feel like family was second priority
when I was a raging, stupid teenager
for not updating you on the important things in life
for going against all of the advice you gave me
spitefully.
I'm sorry.
I'm sorry.
I beg for your forgiveness.

- You told me one day I would regret it and now I
  understand why...

Anger
and
Bargaining

Melanie Ann Vangas

For a moment I thought
get pregnant.
That'll buy me 9 months, at least.
I know you'd want to meet him/her.

For a moment I thought
go back to school.
That'll buy me two years.
I know you'd want to watch me
walk for my diploma.

For a moment I thought
get hired where you reigned territory.
Surely, they would hire Anna's prodigy.
I know you'd want to mentor me.

For a moment I thought
go to the doctors,
find something wrong.
Maybe God would have listened when I
graciously pleaded
"Please let me do this for her."

I know you'd want to set an example for me
to fight for my life.
For a moment
for many moments
for every
single
moment
my mind, lost and fruitless…
I thought…

and then I realized it was in God's hands.

- Buying time is not the same as forever (and I need you)

I have convinced myself that

when
you
die
I
will
too.

So now the question is

how?

- Suicidal.

It's like there was a sudden rush
to accomplish
whatever I dreamt of.

So you were able to see me in the glory
both you and I
knew I possessed.

It wasn't fair.
I felt like I had one day to make it big.
To make you proud.
To be satisfied with our lifetime together.

- Cheated out of a lifetime with you.

Melanie Ann Vangas

God and I have always had a relationship.

I never felt the need to go to church.

I simply felt him crawling through my bones
and I always made it a point
to pray through the sunshine
just as much as I prayed through the rain.

So these days I felt particularly close.
I felt close and I felt home.
And I strangely felt "unlucky"
because this was not *luck*, this was **faith**.

- I am not religious; I am spiritual.

"I know you're asking the same thing I am...how am I supposed to live without her?"

- Papa.

Melanie Ann Vangas

As I write this I can't form poetic prose and so my mind is rambling. It's rambling about the negatives, which I shouldn't be thinking about. I should be clinging to hope and positivity as optimists live longer and so will you live longer if I stay positive? You are beating the odds. You have proven every doctor wrong but still as I sit here unable to write poetic prose, I cry. I cry and I cry and I cry and I cry and I cry and I scream and I cry. What has happened is so unfair. You now wear this precious, diamond, ticking time bomb around your neck around your lungs. How is this life? And who will be there to plan my wedding? At this point can I even fathom having one without your taste, with out your approval, without your negotiations. And who will be there to plan my baby shower? Can I even fathom raising children having to explain the memory of you? The greatest woman I have ever known? And who will plan my finances? As I've listened to your lectures but never took notes because I just assumed you'd be walking into Charles Schwab with me? I say Charles Schwab and I know you are laughing because Papa is a Fidelity kind of guy and yet again I have picked your side. My girl. And who will dress me for my

interviews? Prepare me to negotiate a salary? And who
will help me plant a garden? And who will help me buy
my first home? And who will help me over come my
insecurities? And who will help me understand that friends
grow apart? And who will help me decorate my family
room or living room or even explain to me what the hell
the difference is? And who will remind me which side of
the plate the small fork goes on? And who will send me
care packages full of Neutrogena face wash, Dove body
soap, detergent, sponges, dish soap, Snuggle, essentials etc
etc etc? And who will keep me up to date with the gossip?
Who will help me create a baby book? Who will teach me
how to organize and label my kitchen? Who will teach me
the proper way to vacuum or cook a chicken or mop my
floors or fold my fitted sheets? Who will come over on
Sundays to help me with laundry? Who will help me
through my marital fights? Who will help me plan events?
Who will give me home remedies when I, and everyone in
my home is sick? Who will help me with invites....with
fashion...with interior design...with illness...with loss?

-   Life.

Melanie Ann Vangas

I begged and begged

and begged

for him to grant my wish

of trading places with you.

Like somehow by the grace of God

he'd infect me

and heal you

overnight.

I wish I could do this for you.

I wish I could do this for you...

- You don't deserve this.

Rage.
It sparks within me,
knowing I am part of a generation,
"the millennials"
who will find a cure,
who will find a reason,
to keep sick people like you, here forever.

I am hot and angry as a
fire engulfing the west coast.

Where was this solution when we needed it the most?

- I need you the most.

Melanie Ann Vangas

Making sense of this life is a little hard for me at the moment. Like I'm supposed to go to work knowing that my days with you are numbered? Then again, holding that sort of resentment towards life isn't fair because shit, my days could be numbered but knowing that yours are stamped makes it especially hard to wake up in the morning. How is this right? That I must go earn an honest living in a position I hate while you are home in bed counting your breaths and all I want to do is be with you? What is the purpose and is this the right thing? I find myself constantly trying to put myself in the shoes of our disastrous aftermath and I can't decide what I find right and what is wrong. What is going to help me sleep at night. In fact, I do not sleep anymore and I actually know the answer to that. I should be with you. Life will allow that, I know it. But until then I will stay right here and stick to my schedule and normalcy because I feel like that's what everyone wants.

- A rock and a hard place.

I walked in at the wrong time.

Your son
laying,
crying over you.
Begging for forgiveness.

So preventable (it was).
So apologetic (he was).
So therapeutic (it was).
So damaged (he was).

- I wish he did not have to learn this way.

Melanie Ann Vangas

What happens if this was exactly like you anticipated?
What happens if this was all for a reason?
What if this will bring our family closer?
And teach us to stop creating space between the 6 of us?
But what if it's not?
What if this is just some messed up part of life?

It's easy to believe in God,
believe in anything
at a time of desperation.

But at the end of the day,
scientifically
the chances are slim.

‑ I met someone who told me to think scientifically.

Depression
Loneliness
Reflection

Melanie Ann Vangas

I spent 50 minutes of every hour
with an oxygen monitor
at the tip of your pointer finger.

90 and above.

Thank

you,

Lord.

- Vitals.

I didn't want to leave your side.
In fact, your heart
and my heart
were planting my feet
in the comfort of your guest room,
in the comfort of your basement.
Wherever I fit, really.

My mind turned
on how to survive
without the job I hated
because
I needed
to be
close to you.
I would have died if I weren't.

How majestic it is
to feel your blood
pumping through
   my veins.

- We are one.

Melanie Ann Vangas

Most days I cry and my brain is foggy

because I know you cry and your brain is foggy,

but you will never let us know it.

You are far too vain
no,

you are far too strong
(remember that)

to accept defeat.
   (I'll remember that, too.)

- Empathy.

Google said

You'd stop eating (check).
You'd drink less (check).
You'd see people who have passed (check).
You'd hallucinate (check).
You'd stop going to the bathroom (check).
You'd sleep

  and sleep

    and sleep

(check).

To look out for the pattern between breaths.

That's when I knew you were
Painfully close.

- 8 seconds went by before your chest rose and sunk
  again.

Melanie Ann Vangas

They hadn't seen you in years.
Some, since the holidays.

So dark,
so weak,
breaking at the bones.

But for us
it was victory to see you smiling.
hear your laugh,
hear your greeting,
hear your stories.

We saw progress
while they kneeled beside your bed and prayed.

Something about that made me angry.
I'm not saying it was fair.

But something about them making you feel like
that was a final farewell

Enraged me.
-   No one knows you like we do.

I hurt because
my quiet lips
attempt to express to my superiors
that my grandmother is in need of my presence.

I am surrounded by
lonely people
with no family values.

They do not accept this excuse
for my lack of
e v e r y t h i n g
life
existence
ambition.

You are more than just my grandmother.
You are my best friend.

- How do I explain to co-workers that you are my life
  line?

Melanie Ann Vangas

I remember the last time
we were outside together.
Sitting at a table ordering wine.
Pinot Grigio.
You ordered as you normally do
but ate as little as possible.
We boxed mussels
and fried calamari
and cole slaw
and a cesar salad
(minus two bites).
Afterwards,
the breeze kissed our faces,
the tips of our noses,
our cheeks,
our toes.
As we rolled you in your transporter
down the water view.
I will never forget your laughter
or the sound of your
i n h a l e
and the sight of you
huddled into my grandfather.
- Between Bahrs & South Amboy.

I found myself scrambling
            under beds.
Wreaking havoc
            through closets.
Rummaging
            through documents and bills.

In the attic.
In the office.
In your bedroom.

For photos,
handwriting,
cards.
videos.

Just to piece together important messages.

- Tattoo ideas.

Melanie Ann Vangas

I close my eyes and lay my head down at night.
You would think I'd be anxious but,
for some reason I am not afraid that
you won't be there in the morning
because I know our souls are connected
and mine whispers for yours through the night
and they buzz amongst each other
memories or dreams
of laughter and our cuddles
of movie nights and baking lessons
of birthday parties and cake
surprises
congratulatory toasts.
My sleeping heart feels the sensational vibration.
Your heart beat
beating
and I know you are safe.
I know you are safe
as long as I am here with you.

- I will never leave your side.

I think watching someone slowly lose their spouse is the
most torturous
painful
humbling experience.

Sadness
Greif
Guilt
Resentment
Sorrow
Cherishing
Admiration
Peace
Genuine love
Happiness.

- The stages of watching someone lose their other half.

Melanie Ann Vangas

I know what it's like..
to have a sister you cannot live without.
A ying to your yang.
A second half of your soul.

I know what it's like to feel like
you cannot live without this sister.
You must have felt so safe with her by your side.
Big sisters never let bad things happen to you.

I know what it's like
to have called for her in the middle of the night
to ensure that your heart was still beating
and you were still breathing.
Feeling so much love.
You see, there's power in that.

I know what it's like
to feel that if you *had* to die,
you'd want it to be in your sisters arms.

- Sista, Sista.

52 Sundays

Every time you took a bite

I noticed that you would close your eyes.

I couldn't help when empathy consumed me.

I knew you were trying to take it all in.

The taste, the smell, the texture.

Those are some of the things

you will miss

the most.

- I wonder what you want to bring with you to the next world.

Life really gets to me.
This is really getting to me.
This wine is starting to get to me.
I've started using mail for coasters
like a sloppy, classic bachelor.

I am thirstier than ever.
Wine is the only thing that will make me smile.
Allow
me
to
feel.

- Vice.

52 Sundays

I miss your food.
Your rice and beans.
Your tostones.
The smell of french toast in the morning,
topped with delicate sprinkles of cinnamon
and confection sugar.
Canadian syrup.

I miss your honey mustard.

And my favorite meal of them all...

⁻ Chicken cutlets, mashed potatoes and cream of corn.

The strange part about life is

God put so much thought and effort
into everything about you.
Your mannerisms,
the color of your eyes,
your sense of humor.
The path you have chosen.
The lives you have touched.

Just
to
take it all away.

- The morbidity of existence.

52 Sundays

Today I walked over to the ocean.
Something about the sand and salt water
that cleanses not just my lungs
but my mind.
My heart.

It is remarkable
to witness with my own eyes
such a breath taking view.
Abyss.

It is here that I find God.
This iridescence is impossible without him.
Mother Nature is no one,
as I am no one without him.

The beach is a gift that is carefully placed
footsteps from my door
in this lifetime.
How lucky are we
to be able to come here at no expense
to cry about our grandmothers.

- Long Island.

A weeping willow.

My journal.

As the sun kisses my knee caps.

- I want to get lost for days.

Who you are now

has stained my memory.

I find myself struggling,

desperately clinging to distant memories

to remember who you were before all of this.

- My Mama.

Wondering

gives me anxious answers

to questions

I truly do not want to know the answer to.

-   Will you miss me when you become a star in the sky?

Trivial.
Everything about life is trivial at the moment.

I start to question why it is not normal
to give birth,
raise a family,
live in a village with your own family.
Spend every moment with your family.
Until you die.
Money means nothing.
Make the most of every single moment.
With the people who matter.

- I'm panicking. Why is life so vague?

Melanie Ann Vangas

At times I feel doubtful

and fearful of

being so literal.

But what is deeper?
More passionate?
More meaningful

than the truth?

- Stage fright // Publishing.

Time.
Time.
Time.
What a fragile concept.
I cannot sleep tonight thinking of the
intricate values of time.

It's always too much.
It's never enough.

- Infinity should exist.

Suddenly, I wish I would have taken that job.

Finished that degree.

Dumped that girl.

Made that move.

Invested that money.

Put your sole opinion on a pedestal.

- Shouldacouldawoulda (it's too late).

I called you today.

I cried when we hung up.

You could barely hear me.

I read somewhere on a hospice website
that when you start losing your senses
is when you're on your way out.

 -   I wanted to scream for you.

In which life

do we get to live happily

ever

after?

- I pray I die and wake up your granddaughter again.

Wouldn't it be nice
to know everything you have ever thought of;
store it away on some USB,
pull out the files when I run into a dilemma,
when I run into need,
when I run into happiness.

I am going to need you throughout it all…

- Wouldn't it be nice?

Hues of pink and yellow.

The tone of your voice.

Bright

and cheery.

- Beautiful.

7:00 AM
You wake up grateful.
You are overwhelmed with joy and gratitude.
Energized and determined.
11:00 AM
Midday is near
and the fact that another one is not promised
is starting to take a toll on you.
3:00 PM
You succumb to fear .
Anxiety gets the best of you.
I hear it in your voice,
I feel it in your mannerisms,
you start to shut down.

- Sunrise, sunset.

Lately I enjoy the rain.

It gives me a reason to feel

this agonizing, gaping hole in my chest.

- Approaching.

Upward
Turn

give her greens
give her water
like a plant, she must grow
right?

give her food
give her give her vitamins
like a plant, she must grow
right?

talk to her, gently
whisper courage to her mind
like a plant, she must grow
right?

give her movement
give her sunlight
like a plant, she must grow

right?
…right?

-   I'd do anything. Desperation.

I have so much to thank you for.
But right now
most importantly
I want to thank you for
the relationships
the ties
the love
your best friend
her family
my cousins, aunts, uncles.

I want to thank you for the connections
that have gracefully formed
stronger between us and them.
I (suddenly) don't know who or where
I'd be without these people.

I see why you love them.
I want to love them
endlessly.
But I want you to be here
to love them
forever and always too.
- You are the glue that holds everyone together.

Melanie Ann Vangas

I'm remembering Pennsylvania
and how proud you were of your home.
I was in awe every time the grand doors opened.

I did so little as wake and sleep.
Everything in between you took care of
because we were your girls.

The three little pigs.

You prepared breakfast
and lunch and dinner and snacks.
You prepared popcorn.
You provided music
and the good times.

The walks, the swims, the skiing, the boat rides.

You were much too afraid to sit
in the back of a canoe.

Except you would do it for us.
Your granddaughters.

To see us smile.
Afterwards you would reach into a bag
that you carefully prepared
full of water
and sandwiches
and chips
and love.

- I mean it. How am I going to live without you?

Melanie Ann Vangas

Butterflies.
Hilariously, we both know that
I am petrified of them.
Yet recently I find myself flocked by butterflies.
Mostly Monarchs.

I wonder if they're here to retrieve you
and advise me that
the next time I see a monarch,
not to be afraid.

For it is you, wrapping your wings around me.

- Thinking of signs before necessary.

Your sister spoke to the word of God
through your ears
through your soul.
At all hours of the night and day.

The Doctors,
they told us to give up on you.
To let you go.

But you became incandescent.

So much so
you even started sweating under your blankets
and asking for water to cool down.

- Body temperature / I believe in miracles.

Melanie Ann Vangas

The bed was cold
and sterile.

I managed to contort my body enough
so I could lie perfectly beside you.

Though faint,
your breath
and heartbeat

still
felt
like
home.

- Who knew you could cuddle in the hospital?

52 Sundays

Last night as I wrote
I drank a bottle of red,
my grip tight around its neck…
I cried for you.

I told myself if my poetry does not
shatter my soul to pieces
then I am not digging deep enough.
The Nile river in all of its splendor
flowed through my soul
up my gut, up my throat
and made its way down my eyeballs.

I was satisfied.
It was therapeutic, really.

But then you called in the morning.
Urgently.
To ask if I was okay…

and I don't remember the last time you even picked up the
phone.

- Either we're soulmates or you're psychic.

Melanie Ann Vangas

My favorite part about all of this
        (if that is even fair to say)
is watching your face light up
as you chose which knitted cap
to wear that day.

Coral
to match that rambunctious,
sharp smile.

-   The cutest little lady.

It's almost like you know I need magic
so you're sending magic my way
in poetry,
in creativity.
I refuse to believe that anything that has
put a smile on my face
was sent by anyone or anything other than you.

\- Coping.

Each tone of her words
I find myself trying to memorize.
I am scared.
I am petrified.
I feel like Titi has to become you once you are gone.
So I spend this time remembering
the tone of her voice
and her laugh
and her ways.

If it can not be you,
I need her.
I need her.
I need her, Mama.

I speak to her and I hear so much of you.
I look her way and see so much of you.
I joke with her and hear you laughing.

Does she know me better than I think she does?

- No one could ever replace you but you two are one in
  the same.

We don't need cold and calculated.

We need genuineness.

You are un-welcome here.

- To those who want to watch us fall.

Melanie Ann Vangas

Joy came from your ecstatic reaction
to your sons cooking.
It must have been both
flattering and surprising
to know that the moments you spent in overalls
in the kitchen
meant something to him.

- He has become quite the chef (though, never as good as you).

You embody eloquence.

I hope to be like you

when I grow up.

- If I get the chance to.

Melanie Ann Vangas

I read books that mention sweet old women
nonchalantly learning technology
and I laugh because it reminds me
of your discovery of FaceTime,
animojis, iMessage.

These memories seem so far but
you're still here.
You're still here.

- You are still here, Amen.

The phone rang

"She isn't going to make it through the night."

Doctors.

They don't know her like we do.

- May 9th.

I try my very best to
picture how to move on without you.
I've managed to convince myself
that I'm prepared for the hit.
My very own
evacuation
rehabilitation
crisis response
emergency
back up
plan.

Some days I 'm okay.
Most days, I am not.

- Self help.

Reconstruction
and
Working
Through

Melanie Ann Vangas

He wipes the counter
and we chuckle behind our teeth.
You know and I know
that he is learning slowly how to
manage without you.
So he does things like wipe the counter
three or four times
and requests your approval.
Though this image often brings me to tears,
we chuckle
because we cannot believe he is becoming
slightly domesticated.

Who would have thought?
Papa can now make a salad.

- In preparation.

Who am I to call

when my back gets shattered

into a thousand, million, billion pieces?

- My back bone.

I called this morning and you sounded
just like yourself.
"I don't think I'll be able to make it
to work this morning"
you said, in disappointment.
Except you're bedridden
and have been retired for 11 years.
I wanted to correct you but instead,
"I'm all for calling out!
Use your sick time,
that's what it's there for."

A cold reminder that things
will never be the same.

‑ They say at this stage you believe you're places that
  once made you happy.

My dreams have become repetitive.

I trace the image of your smile

and your frail legs,

your chipmunk cheeks (ha),

the texture of your hair.

It has become my favorite Cadence.

- I will never forget you.

One of the most interesting things about
all of this
was noticing your ability to forgive.

You spread nothing but light and love.

An eerie, calm and serene demeanor flooded me
as I realized you were genuinely at peace.

You ask for people you normally would not have
and enjoyed their company,
their dialogue,
their well wishes.

Part of me hated this
for the simple fact that the light at the end
of the tunnel became more dim.
Part of me admired this
because I knew how prideful you were.
It was selfless of you.

-   It is certainly "goodbye" not "see you later".

The evening comes

and your scent lingers.

My God, I am going to miss you.

\-   Phantosmia.

Sister
Friend
Cousin
Niece
Nephew
Aunt
Uncle
God children

All of them.
Everyone.
Do you see how regal you are?

- Matriarch.

You encouraged me.
Somehow guided
my very presence on this earth
to be the best it could be.

Through yoga
and St. Johns Warts
organic food
and holy water.

- Holistically, the best me because of you.

You have made a profound impact on this world.

It shows in the cars lined up

on your street

followed by the chime of your doorbell

and the hum of your ringtone

as you lie in your bed.

⁃   Queen.

Acceptance
and
Hope

Pen to paper.
I try to think of anything that I want to be sure
I say to you.
When it comes down to that dreaded moment
I think I will just whisper that
I love you.
I'll always need you.
Please visit.
Stay with me for a lifetime.
I can't wait to see you again.
I'll be sure to live how you wanted me to.

- Planned goodbye.

How disgusting and unforgiving it would be
to live my worst life everyday
in honor of you.

- I must live on for the both of us.

I would hope you'd come to me often.
In butterflies, in words, in dreams.
In paranormal signs.
In love.
Through people.
However it may be.
I think I will be okay
if I always felt you by my side.

- The rainbow bridge.

52 Sundays

You watch us grow

from the branches you stretched to us.

I hope you are pleased

with the bark of our skin

and the roots in our soil.

For we live to make you proud.

- Following your footsteps.

The texts stopped coming.
The calls stopped coming.
The visits came to a screeching halt.

And in the end

there was just the six of us.

- Vangas.

My only wish is that
the stairway to heaven has
pink roses wrapped around it's beams.
And cardinals.
And Pinot Grigio
waiting for you.

- Only the best for the best.

Melanie Ann Vangas

I hope that when you close your eyes
For the last time
you remember just how
special
you
are.

I love you.

Made in the USA
San Bernardino,
CA